THIS BOOK IS THE SEVENTH IN HARPER & ROW'S NATIVE AMERICAN PUBLISHING PROGRAM. ALL PROFITS FROM THIS PROGRAM ARE USED TO SUPPORT PROJECTS DESIGNED TO AID THE NATIVE AMERICAN PEOPLE.

OTHER BOOKS IN THE PROGRAM

Seven Arrows, by Hyemeyohsts Storm

Ascending Red Cedar Moon, by Duane Niatum

Winter in the Blood, by James Welch

Indians' Summer, by Nas'Naga

Carriers of the Dream Wheel, edited by Duane Niatum

Riding the Earthboy 40, by James Welch

GOING FOR THE RAIN

Poems by
Simon J. Ortiz

GOING
FOR THE RAIN

HARPER & ROW, PUBLISHERS

New York   Hagerstown   San Francisco   London

Grateful acknowledgment is made to the following in which
some of the poems first appeared:

Dacotah Territory: "The Creation, According to Coyote;"
"Four Poems for a Child Son;" and "Crossing the Colorado
River into Yuma."
Greenfield Review: "The Expectant Father," "The Poet;"
"The Wisconsin Horse;" and "To Insure Survival."
Indian Historian: "Travels in the South: East Texas, The
Creek Nation East of the Mississippi, Crossing the Georgia
Border into Florida" and "I Told You I like Indians."
The Way by Stan Steiner and Shirley Hill Witt, Alfred A.
Knopf, Inc. "Relocation" and "Missing That Indian Name
of Roy or Ray."
Pembroke Magazine: "Hunger in New York City" originally
appeared under the title "Hunger in New York."
Sol Tide: "Buzzard" and "Dry Root in a Wash."
Yardbird Reader: "Forming Child."

Library of Congress Cataloging in Publication Data
Ortiz, Simon J   1941–
Going for the rain.
Poems.
I.   Title.
PS3565.R77G6   811'.5'4   76–8707
ISBN 0–06–451511–7
ISBN 0–06–451512–5 pbk.

FIRST EDITION

Designed by Christine Aulicino

FOR JOY:

For the meaning that is possible—
With all my love

Contents

Prologue

There is a song which goes like this:

> Let us go again, brother; let us go for the shiwana.
> Let us make our prayer songs.
> We will go now. Now we are going.
> We will bring back the shiwana.
> They are coming now. Now, they are coming.
> It is flowing. The plants are growing.
> Let us go again, brother; let us go for the shiwana.

A man makes his prayers; he sings his songs. He considers all that is important and special to him, his home, children, his language, the self that he is. He must make spiritual and physical preparation before anything else. Only then does anything begin.

A man leaves; he encounters all manners of things. He has adventures, meets people, acquires knowledge, goes different places; he is always looking. Sometimes the travelling is hazardous; sometimes he finds meaning and sometimes he is destitute. But he continues; he must. His travelling is a prayer as well, and he must keep on.

A man returns, and even the returning has moments of despair and tragedy. But there is beauty and there is joy. At times he is confused, and at times he sees with utter clarity. It is all part of the travelling that is a prayer. There are things he must go through before he can bring back what he seeks, before he can return to himself.

The rain comes and falls. The shiwana have heeded the man, and they have come. The man has brought back the rain. It falls, and it is nourishing. The man returns to the strength that his selfhood is, his home, people, his language, the knowledge of who he is. The cycle has been travelled; life has beauty and meaning, and it will continue because life has no end.

THE FIRST:

PREPARATION

THE CREATION, ACCORDING TO COYOTE

"First of all, it's all true."
Coyote, he says this, this way,
humble yourself, motioning and meaning
what he says.

You were born when you came
from that body, the earth;
your black head burst from granite,
the ashes cooling,

until it began to rain.
It turned muddy then,
and then green and brown things
came without legs.

They looked strange.
Everything was strange.
There was nothing to know then,

until later, Coyote told me this,
and he was b.s.-ing probably,
two sons were born,
Uyuyayeh and Masaweh.

They were young then,
and then later on they were older.

And then the people were wondering
what was above.
They had heard rumors.

But, you know, Coyote,
he was mainly bragging
when he said (I think),
"My brothers, the Twins then said,
'Let's lead these poor creatures
and save them.'"

And later on, they came to light
after many exciting and colorful
and tragic things of adventure;
and this is the life, all these, all these.

My uncle told me all this, that time.
Coyote told me too, but you know
how he is, always talking to the gods,
the mountains, the stone all around.

And you know, I believe him.

FORMING CHILD

April 1973

1ST ONE

O child's tremble
against your mother's innerwall,
is a true movement
without waste or hesitation,
a beating of wings
following ancient trails
to help us return.

2ND ONE

I will point
out your place on the earth,
among mountains, on ground,
by old watercourses, in wind,
where your mother walked,
where her mother walked.

This way then,
This way,
I will show you those points
where you will present yourself.

Two days ago
when I was at the foot
of Black Mountain,
there were rain clouds forming
in a space
between the tip of the mountain
and a point in the sky.
Two days before that,
I saw a hawk circling
in a slow, cool wind
south of that place
where I stood watching.

4TH ONE

Years ago, your brother and I
walked from Chee Goodluck's hogan
in the Lukachukai Mountains
to a place where water flowed
from under huge granite boulders.
The water tasted like the wind,
roots, fresh herbs, sweet smells.

5TH ONE

I want you to see a pass
in the Chuska Mountains
where there are aspen, oak,
elevation high enough
for fir and snow
enough to last till June.
I've been up there twice,
once on a hard winter day.

6TH ONE

Among the things I would require
of you is that you should relish
the good wheat bread your mother makes,
taking care that you should think
how her hands move, kneading the dough,
shaping it with her concern,
and how you were formed and grew in her.

7TH ONE

Near the Summit, SE of Kinlichee,
I saw a piece of snowmelt water
that I thought would look good
on a silver bracelet with maybe
two small turquoise stones at its sides;
but then, I liked the way it was, too,
under pine trees, the snow feeding it,
the evening sunlight slanting off it,
and I knew that you would understand
why I decided to leave it like that.

8TH ONE

Yesterday, as I was lighting a cigarette,
Raho warned me with,
"If anyone starts a fire,
Smokey the Bear will come put them out."
Bear's got a lot of friends.

FOUR POEMS FOR A CHILD SON

December 18, 1972

"WHAT'S YOUR INDIAN NAME?"

It has to do with full moments
of mountains, deserts, sun, gods,
song, completeness.

It has to do with stories, legends
full of heroes and travelling.

It has to do with rebirth and growing
and being strong and seeing.

You see it's like this (the movement) :
go to the water
and gather the straight willow stems
bring them home
work carefully at forming them
tie on the feathers
paint them with the earth
feed them and talk with them
pray.

You see, son, the eagle is a whole person
the way it lives; it means it has to do
with paying attention to where it is,
not the center of the earth especially
but part of it, one part among all parts,
and that's only the beginning.

It Was The Third Day, July 12, 1971

Hitch-hiking on the way to Colorado,
I heard your voice, "Look, Dad . . ."
                    A hawk
sweeping its wings
                    clear

through the whole sky

                    the blue
                    the slow wind
fresh with the smell of summer alfalfa
at the foot of the Jemez Mountains.

(You see, the gods come during the summer
for four days amongst the people,
bring gifts, bring hope and life,
you can see them, I mean.)

Waiting for my next ride,
I sang,
        Look, the plants with bells.
        Look, the stones with voices.

Yesterday

In the late afternoon,
there was suddenly a noise of birds
filling up everything.

This morning in the newspaper,
I read about starlings at the Air Force base.

I guess they were but all I knew yesterday
was that they filled up the trees,
the utility wires, the sky, the world.

That's all I know.

Respect your mother and father.
Respect your brothers and sisters.
Respect your uncles and aunts.
Respect your land, the beginning.
Respect what is taught you.
Respect what you are named.
Respect the gods.
Respect yourself.
Everything that is around you
is part of you.

THE EXPECTANT FATHER

I am an expectant father.

Pray then:
smile for all good things,
note the wind,
note the rain,
touch the gentleness with care;
be good.

After we had watched the hawk circling in the hot wind
and lost it against the color of the mesa across the
valley, we decided to climb down the mesa to this
spring. We walked for about half a mile and finally
arrived there. The spring is in a cave made by two huge
slabs of sandstone cliff leaning into each other. The
water dripped from soft crumbly shale and ran into a
small pool. Around the water were handhigh green
ferny plants and moss grew on stone. There were move-
ments in the water which were our reflections and the
tiny water beings that lived there. Earl dipped into
the water with a rusty can and drank and then Gilly.

It was my turn then. The spring water tasted sweet and
like a dark underground cavern, but something of a
taste that was more like a touching wind than anything
else. There was something else too, something else. We
were quite young then. We weren't so tired and hot
after a while anymore, and we climbed on down to the
flat valley and looked somemore for our horses.

When the child comes, expectant father,
tell the child.

When I have awoken in the early mornings,
I have felt the child's flutter at the small of my back,
the mother's belly pressed against me.
The child is a butterfly cupped in the Mother's hands.
Be gentle, Naya; be kind, this morning
and for all mornings of our—your children's—lives.

When it rains in a soft wind,
it feels so good.

TO INSURE SURVIVAL

for Rainy Dawn
born July 5, 1973

You come forth
the color of a stone cliff
at dawn,
changing colors,
blue to red
to all the colors of the earth.

Grandmother Spider speaks
laughter and growing
and weaving things
and threading them

together to make life
to wear;
all these, all these.

You come out, child,
naked as that cliff at sunrise,
shorn of anything
except spots of your mother's blood.
You just kept blinking your eyes
and trying to catch your breath.

In five more days,
they will come,
singing, dancing,
bringing gifts,
the stones with voices,
the plants with bells.
They will come.

Child, they will come.

LANGUAGE

*"The Word is sacred to a
child."—N. Scott Momaday,*
House Made of Dawn

I carried my baby daughter to her bed,
laid her down; she turned her head aside,
and I patted her back, murmured a singsong,
and she fell asleep making small universal sounds.

Later she calls out—
from the next room—
go to pick her up—
she is so warm
a young animal—movement—

take her before the long
mirror—say Rainy, Rainy
murmur sound—she reaches
her hand—meets her own
hand—hand meets mirrored
hand—she smiles at my
mirrored face—what
does she think?

What is it, the murmur, the song of a chant,
drawn out holler, deep caress in the throat,
the wind searching hillside ledge?

The language of movements—sights—
possibilities and impossibilities—
pure existence—which leap into exact
moments—keep being there all the time—
static quality needing nothing else—
being its only validity—
adequate unto itself—solid—
to know it one has to become a part
of it—a word is the poem—child
upon hearing a sound hears the poem
of hearing—original motion of it
is complete—sanctified—the sphere
of who he or she is who is hearing
the poetry—motion of inwards a drawn
breath—complete entity of sound/word
has its own energy and motion.

Rainy sound is something like, "Uh oh"
motion of air, muscles,
tiny soft bones in upper chest,
mouth opening, moist cavern,
symbol of her beginning word,
pucker lips into,
"Where do sounds come from?"

From the deep well
where all points meet
and intercross again
and countless times
again.

The throat sound
knows its intercrossings;
the first sound,
it overflows and touches me.

She whimpers another sound,
meaning,
"What is it? What shall I do
for you, child?"
comes from me, an extension
of herself.

I listened to the wind yesterday,
another sound. Travels
into me. Purpose: be simple
and thoughtful, flowing
with a singular pulsing.
All language comes forth
outward from the center. Hits
the curve of your being. Fits

    —"chiseled" occurs to me
       out of an unremembered passage
       in some book, has to do
       with image required to remember
       or remembered; "chiseled"
       into mind or memory stone—

into thoughts of sound itself,
the energy it is
and the motion inherent in it.

FOUR BIRD SONGS

FIRST SONG

Is a little wind
fledgling
nestled
in mountain's crooked finger,

is a river
into a secret place
that shows everything,
little song.

In your breath,
hold this seed
only a while
and seek with it.

One single universe,
I
am
only a little.

SECOND SONG

The sound
in wood,
a morning hollowness
of a cave on the flank of a small hill

startles
with its moan,
yearning,
a twitch of skin.

In the distant place,
a wind starts
coming here,
a waiting sound.

It is here now.
Shiver.
You are rewarded
for waiting.

THIRD SONG

By breathing he started
into the space
before him
and around him,

cleared his throat,
said this song
maybe tomorrow
is for rain.

Lightly
hummed
a tight leathersound
and then heavily.

It rained
the next day,
and he sang
another song for that.

FOURTH SONG

An old stone
was an old blue,
spotted,
the egg's shell,

only moments before
under the sun
that had become new
against old sand.

A tear falling,
stirring into space,
filling it completely,
making new space.

When he touched it,
and it moved,
it was still warm
with that life.

TIME AND MOTION AND SPACE

I told Barbara,
"When I was a kid
we used to throw rocks
off the cliffedges at Acu.
We were fascinated
because the falling of rock
seems to be something
like stopping time.

I mean it seems real
and clear to you then.
Time is so deep, fathomless,
and all the *time*
that you can't pin it down
at exact points
nor with explanations.
But being witness
to falling rock. . . .
Time is tangible then.
It is a rock falling
from the release of your hand,
moving into, through, down
space to the ground
at bottom cliffedge.
That's how you know then.

Time and motion and space:
pine and fir,
the wind,
lichen on sunwarm flat rock,
a road below in the valley,
voices of friends,
ourselves.
"Pine song," she said.
Butterfly comes by.
And then Bee all dressed
in bright yellow and black.

"This is the way it is."

"I'm not just making it up."

BUCK NEZ

*a birthday pup present for
me from friends; I was
taking him home for my son.*

Ten miles
the other side of Nageezi,
we stopped
a mile south of the highway.

I built a fire big enough
to signal the gods.

You slept against my neck,
curled by my soul. Once,
I awoke to a tiny whimper,
and I worried
that I should feed you
when I had nothing to eat
myself.

[17]

It rained that night,
and it got cold.

In the morning,
I woke up to find
a puppy, you, yapping
like the original life,
a whole mystery crying
for sustenance.

We prayed.

What I want is a full life
for my son,
for myself,
for my Mother,
the Earth.

THE POET

"Are you really a poet?"

"Shore."

Crickets always talk like that.

A couple nights after,
I listened for a long time
to a couple reminding themselves
about 10 million years ago
in some cave in Asia.
It was a long, long time ago.
They rattled membranes together
and sang all night long.

"I didn't know you were a poet."

Later on,
there was another cave.
A woman was moaning,
and later she was laughing,
not very far from a glacier's edge.
To the south were swaying grasses,
brightly colored birds, warm oceans,
hot deserts, and strange gods
who demanded nothing.

She asked me if I liked crickets.
I said, "Yeah, but not cockroaches."
I wondered out loud
if cockroaches are any relation
to crickets, and she said, "Maybe,
but not too close."
I want to look it up somewhere,
but ten million years
is a hell of a long time
to really clear it up.

"How long you been a cricket?"

MY FATHER'S SONG

Wanting to say things,
I miss my father tonight.
His voice, the slight catch,
the depth from his thin chest,
the tremble of emotion
in something he has just said
to his son, his song:

We planted corn one Spring at Acu—
we planted several times
but this one particular time
I remember the soft damp sand
in my hand.

My father had stopped at one point
to show me an overturned furrow;
the plowshare had unearthed
the burrow nest of a mouse
in the soft moist sand.

Very gently, he scooped tiny pink animals
into the palm of his hand
and told me to touch them.
We took them to the edge
of the field and put them in the shade
of a sand moist clod.

I remember the very softness
of cool and warm sand and tiny alive mice
and my father saying things.

TWO WOMEN

She is a Navajo woman sitting at her loom.
The sun is not far up, but she has already prepared
her husband's and sons' breakfasts,
and they have eaten and left.
Today, her husband will pull the weeds
from among the pumpkin, squash, and cornplants
in their small field at the mouth of Redwater Wash.
The two sons have driven their sheep and goats
to the Hill With White Stones. And she is left
in the calm of her work at the loom.

Quickly, Grandmother,
the Spider spins,
quick flips and turns,
the colors.

O the colors, Grandmother,
I saw in the two-days-ago rainbow.

O Grandmother Spider, the sun is shining
through your loom.

She works gently, her skirt flared out,
in the sun of this morning's Summer.

Desbah is grinding corn into meal.
The kernels of the corn are blue
with a small scattering of whites;
they are hard and she can hear them
crack sharply under the handstone
she is using. She reaches into a sack
for the corn and puts them on the stone.
Her father, Silversmith, brought it
one evening to her. He had it tied
on his horse with some rope,
and it was wrapped in some canvas cloth.

As she stops momentarily grinding,
she can hear him again say, "This stone
for the grinding of corn is for my child.
The man who gets her will be pleased,
but he will not like to carry this heavy thing
around," and he had laughed with his love
and hopes for her. Silversmith had gone
on ahead many years ago, and she never did
have a man get her.

She can hear the blue and white kernels
crack sharply on the heavy stone.

POEM FOR JODY ABOUT LEAVING

I was telling you
about the red cliff faces
of the Lukachukai Mountains—
how it is
going away—
and near Tsegi,
the red and brown land
that is like a strong
and a healthy woman
ready to give birth
to many children,
and you don't ever want to go
but do anyway.

THE SECOND:

LEAVING

TOWARDS SPIDER SPRINGS

I was amazed
at the wall of stones
by the roadside.

Our baby, his mother,
and I were trying to find
the right road,
but all we found
were ones deeply rutted
and high centered.
We were trying to find
a place to start all over
but couldn't.

On the way back,
we passed by the
stone walls again.
The stones had no mortar;
they were just stones
balancing against the sky.

ARRIVAL IN SUDDEN SEASIDE
FOG THIS MORNING

Last night travelling
through the barebone desert
parts of Arizona and California,
a variety of discomforts
riding my poor body
through the long-distance night
of Casa Grande, Dateland,
Yuma, El Centro, and now
this morning early,
they have become roadside ghosts
vanished into the sudden fog.

BLUES SONG FOR THE PHOENIX BUS DEPOT DERELICT

Waiting for my bus
that comes in tonight
and then leaves me
sitting here.
Waiting to leave.
Waiting to come.
Please,
I know Phoenix streets
cold gray and hard.
Please,
leave me alone
for tonight.
Sitting here coming and going,
I'm waiting for everything
to arrive
just this one time for me.

MANY FARMS NOTES

taken on a Many Farms,
Arizona trip, Spring 1973

1.

Hawk circles
on wind roads
only he knows
how to follow
to the center.

2.

Hawk's bright eyes
read trees, stones,
points in horizon,

movements, how wind
and shadows play
tricks, and sudden
rabbit flurry
which reminds him
of his empty stomach.

3.

A Tuba City girl asks me
if I ever write from paintings.
I tell her that I write
with visions in my head.

4.

I'm walking out of Gallup.
He calls, "Hey, my fren,
where you going too fas'?"
"Many Farms."
"Good lucks."
I smile for his good thoughts.

5.

A wind vision:
if you look into the Chinle Valley,
you will see the Woman's cover,
a tapestry her Old Mother worked
for 10 million years or so.

6.
On the way south to the junction,
I looked to the northeast
and couldn't decide whether that point
in the distance beyond the Defiance uplift
was Sonsela Butte or Fluted Rock.

7.

The L.A. Kid was a city child
and a Navajo rodeo queen,
who said she'd seen me on the road
coming out of Window Rock,
said her friend had said,
"I think that was him;
we just passed him up,"
and felt so bad,
said she was born in L.A.
but wasn't really a city girl
and visited her homeland
every Summer, and said
her mother was from Lukachukai.

8.

Bear occurs several times, of course:

The day before I went to Many Farms,
received a card from Snyder,
said he'd "spent a day watching grizzly bear"
grizzling at the San Diego Zoo.

Navajo girl had a painting of Bear.
He was facing east and looking up.
A line was drawn through him,
from chest to tail, rainbow muted colors,
and I said, "That line seems to be both
the horizon and the groundline where you start."

She told me about what the people say.
Don't ever whistle at night where bears are,
because female bears do that
when there are courting bears around.
Remember that: don't whistle
in the dark, horny Bear night.

That Navajo girl asked me
what I thought about polygamy.

I told her I thought it was a good idea
but not for keeps, and we laughed.
I wonder how many wives Bear has?

9.

For Monday night supper, we had
mutton ribs, round steak,
good Isleta bread, tortillas,
broccoli, green chili, potatoes,
gravy, coffee, and apple pie.
The mutton was tough and Francis said,
"You gotta be tough
to live on this land."

10.

After I got out of the back
of a red pickup truck,
I walked for about a mile
and met three goats, two sheep and a lamb
by the side of the road.
I was wearing a bright red wool cap
pulled over my ears,
and I suppose they thought I was maybe weird
because they were all ears and eyes.
I said, "Yaahteh, my friends.
I'm from Acoma, just passing through."
The goat with the bell jingled it
in greeting a couple of times.
I could almost hear the elder sheep
telling the younger, "You don't see
many Acoma poets passing through here."

11.

"What would you say that the main theme
  of your poetry is?"
"To put it as simply as possible,
  I say it this way: to recognize
  the relationships I share with everything."

I would like to know well the path
from just east of Black Mountain
to the gray outcropping of Roof Butte
without having to worry
about the shortest way possible.

12.

I worried about two women discussing how
to get rid of a Forming Child
without too much trouble, whether
it would be in the hospital in Gallup
or in Ganado.
Please forgive my worry and my concern.

13.

"Are you going to Gallup, shima?"
"Yes."
"One dollar and fifty cents, please."

OLD HILLS

West of Ocotillo Wells,
the hills are pretty old.
In fact, they're older than any signs
telling tourists where they're at,
older than all of millennium's signpainters.

I was there with a number
of university students.
They were making a film
in the desert about an old Indian
who was burying his daughter,
planting her back into the earth.

The completed film, in color,
worth six semester credit hours,
was about life. The director
was a young Crow man
who had grown up in Los Angeles.

The rocks and cacti tolerate us
very quietly; they probably laugh
softly at us with the subtle chuckle
of ancient humor that our jubilant youth
knows not yet to recognize and share.

Beane, a black youth from Watts,
was adjusting a light meter,
and he had trouble with some figures,
and Doug, the Crow from L.A.,
hollered, "Beane, I don't think you understand
what the hell the sun has to do with your shadow."

These hills are pretty old.
Some have worn down to flat desert valley.
Some stones remember being underwater
and the cool fresh green winds.

21 AUGUST '71 INDIAN

Building the fire,
using shavings I made this afternoon
as I attempted a sculpture, a bird
or the wisp of high thin cloud in Fall,
from a length of curved white pine.
The fire is slow to catch,
wood is damp, but it begins to start,
and I throw on the larger pieces.

An old girlfriend came by a while ago,
fat and getting older,
wearing wide dark glasses;
she held a fat and healthy baby.
I was making tortillas then,
flour on my hands, rolling dough out
on a board with a tall drinking glass.
She didn't say anything
as her husband and I talked;
I was glad she didn't ask why
I was not a lawyer or an engineer.

Fire burns the thin shavings quickly
and soon dies down under larger pieces.
The red coals are weak, have to watch
and put smaller pieces on next time.
Get knife and splinter larger into smaller
and feed the coals, being patient.
Will have a late supper tonight;
maybe the clouds will part some by then
and let me see some stars.

It's been years since.
I told her then of the things
that I was discovering about myself.
I took long evening walks
and listened to the sounds of rivers,
and she would come looking for me.
She never knew, I don't think, until today
that I could make tortillas—
that I've learned to survive this way—
over a fire, for my lone supper.

Fire burns good now, good red coals.
Will get the beans and tortillas
to warm over the glowing coals.
I will have purple plums for dessert.
I am able to see some stars now, too.
I don't think I'll ever be an engineer
or at least even a lawyer.

Hesperus Acoma
Summer 1971

SMALL THINGS TODAY

Had a tortilla with some honey
at midafternoon. It was good.
Wished I had some chili.

Smell of apples, wet fields;
in back of the blue tent
is a box of last season's
Animas Valley apples; soon,
it will be another Fall.

Wind blows, shakes the tarp,
water falls to the ground.
The sound of water splashing.

Several hours ago, watched
a woodpecker watching me.
We both moved our heads
with funny jerks.

Rex and his sad, dog eyes.

Somebody looking around in a field,
looking for lost things.

Notice bean sprouts growing.
They're very pale and nude.

Rex doesn't like chicken livers,
but gizzards are okay.

TRAVELS IN THE SOUTH

1. East Texas

When I left the Alabama-Coushatta people,
it was early morning.
They had treated me kindly, given me food,
spoken me words of welcome, and thanked me.
I touched them, their hands, and promised
I would be back.

When I passed by the Huntsville State Pen
I told the Indian prisoners what the people said
and thanked them and felt very humble.
The sun was rising then.

When I got to Dallas I did not want to be there.
I went to see the BIA Relocation man.
He told me, "I don't know how many Indians
there are in Dallas; they come every week."
I talked with Ray, a Navajo; he didn't have a job,
was looking, and he was a welder.
I saw an Apache woman crying for her lost life.

When it was evening of the next day,
I stopped at a lake called Caddo.
I asked a park ranger, "Who was Caddo?"
And he said it used to be some Indian tribe.

I met two Black women fishing at the lake.
I sat by them; they were good to be with.
They were about seventy years old and laughed,
and for the first and only time in my life
I cut a terrapin's head off because,
as the women said, "They won't let go until sundown."

When it was after sundown in East Texas, I prayed
for strength and the Caddo and the Black women
and my young son at home and Dallas and when
it would be the morning, the sun.

[34]

2. The Creek Nation East of the Mississippi

Once, in a story, I wrote that Indians are everywhere.
Goddamn right.

In Pensacola, Florida, some hotdog stand
operator told me about Chief McGee.

"I'm looking for Indians," I said.
"I know Chief Alvin McGee," he said.
I bought a hotdog and a beer.
"He lives near Atmore, Alabama,
cross the tracks, drive by the school,
over the freeway to Atlanta, about a mile.
He lives at the second house on the right."

I called from a payphone in Atmore.
Mr. McGee told me to come on over.
I found his home right away,
and he came out when I stopped in his yard.
He had a big smile on his face.
I'd seen his face before in the history books
when they bothered to put Creeks in them.

He told me about Osceola.
"He was born in this county," Chief McGee said.
He showed me his garden and fields.
"I have seventy acres," he said.
"We used to have our own school,
but they took that away from us.
There ain't much they don't try to take."

We watched the news on TV.
It was election time in Alabama,
George Wallace against something.
People kept coming over to his house,
wanting the Chief's support. "Wallace is the one."
"Brewer is our man." They kept that up all night.
The next morning the election was on,
but I left right after breakfast.

[35]

Chief Alvin McGee put his arms around me
and blessed me. I remembered my grandfather,
the mountains, the land from where I came,
and I thanked him for his home, "Keep together,
please don't worry about Wallace, don't worry."

I was on that freeway to Atlanta
when I heard about the killings at Kent State.
I pulled off the road just past a sign which read
NO STOPPING EXCEPT IN CASE OF
    EMERGENCY
and hugged a tree.

3. CROSSING THE GEORGIA BORDER INTO FLORIDA

I worried about my hair, kept my car locked.
They'd look at me, lean, white, nervous,
their lips moving, making wordless gestures.

My hair is past my ears.
My Grandfather wore it like that.
He used to wear a hat, a gray one,
with grease stains on it.
The people called him Tall One
because he was tall for an Acoma.

I had a hard time in Atlanta;
I thought it was because
I did not have a suit and tie.
I had to stay at the Dinkler Plaza,
a classy joint, for an Indian meeting.
The desk clerk didn't believe it
when I walked up, requested a room,
towel rolled up under my arm,
a couple books, and my black bag of poems.
I had to tell him who I really wasn't.
He charged me twenty dollars for a room,
and I figured I'm sure glad
that I'm not a Black man,
and I was sure happy to leave Atlanta.

A few miles from the Florida line,
I picked some flowers beside the highway
and put them with the sage I got in Arizona.
After the Florida line, I went to a State Park,
paid two-fifty, and the park ranger told me,
"This place is noted for the Indians
that don't live here anymore."
He didn't know who they used to be.

When I got to my camping site
and lay on the ground,
a squirrel came by and looked at me.
I moved my eyes. He moved his head.
"Brother," I said.
A red bird came, hopped.
"Brother, how are you?" I asked.
I took some bread, white, and kind of stale,
and scattered some crumbs before them.
They didn't take the crumbs,
and I didn't blame them.

RELOCATION

Don't talk me no words.
Don't frighten me
for I am in the blinding city.
The lights,
the cars,
the deadened glares
        tear my heart
        and close my mind.

Who questions my pain,
the tight knot of anger
in my breast?

I swallow hard and often
and taste my spit
and it does not taste good.
Who questions my mind?

I came here because I was tired;
the BIA taught me to cleanse myself,
daily to keep a careful account of my time.
Efficiency was learned in catechism;
the nuns spelled me God in white.
And I came here to feed myself—
corn, potatoes, chili, and mutton
did not nourish me they said.

So I agreed to move.
I see me walking in sleep
down streets, down streets gray with cement
and glaring glass and oily wind,
armed with a pint of wine
I cheated my children to buy.
I am ashamed.
I am tired.
I am hungry.
I speak words.
I am lonely for hills.
I am lonely for myself.

BUSRIDE CONVERSATION

She says,
"I came to Albuquerque
on Wednesday."

She's about eighteen.

"I have three shell necklaces
ready to sell.
A man offered me thirty dollars."

She smells slightly sour
with sweat, the several nights
in Albuquerque.

We mention names
to each other,
people we know,
places we've been.

She says, "In May,
I was in Gallup jail
with a girl from Acoma."

I've been there too.

"The cook was an Apache.
He sneaked two chiliburgers
into us.
He was sure good to us."

She giggles, and I laugh.
She gets off at Domingo Junction.

"Be good," I say.

"You too," she says.

PORTRAIT OF A POET WITH A CONSOLE TV IN HAND

I bought that TV at John's TV
on College Avenue in San Diego
and lugged it all the way home
on the Greyhound bus.

Sitting in Phoenix bus depot
waiting room, TV sitting on my lap,
I felt foolish as I watched
depot officials grab an old man
derelict as he searched dazedly
into an open locker compartment.
They pushed him reeling out
into deadly stunning American city.
At 12:30 A.M., there wasn't anything else on,
just that already too late, late channel.

I had known that I would be coming home
but the TV-in-hand bit
was an entirely new angle, and I think
that it must have to do with an odd madness.

SURPRISE

On Friday we passed
through mountains,
through place called Alpine,
handlettered signs
on apple cider roadside stands,
a small lake, lots of pine
and higher up twisted aspen
made me lonesome for Crystal
on Arizona-New Mexico line.

Yesterday, it snowed
only seventy miles southeast
of San Diego in the Cuyamac Mtns.
Monday morning, I am very clear
in my head—realize
I didn't get drunk all weekend.
Surprises, I like to learn
from them when I am clear.

EARLY MORNING

One knows
some instinctive response
to movements.

Shadowed murmurs,
softly, softly
go away.
The faintest quiver
at the edge
of awakedness.
Quiet, child,
my soul—
don't move now,
not yet.
Wait just a while.

I heard streetsweepers
at least three times
early this morning.
Now, I wonder
if they were
only occurrences
in my dreams.

The other times
there was more silence
than I have ever felt
in the streets before.
Acres and acres
of silence.

Where was the moon?

MAKING AN ACQUAINTANCE

I walk outside without my shoes
on searing hot asphalt front yard.
Howard, my new landlord, says,
"It's gonna be a bitch of a Summer."
Strange, I think, what words mean.
He has a tanned middle-aged face,
used to be in real estate in Ohio,
sold his business and moved West.
We get acquainted by talking
about the coming Summer.
"Yeah," I agree with him,
"it's gonna be a bitch."
My feet are burning for coolness.

WITHOUT YOU

What to do without you
is night madness.

Once you called up,
"I was crossing the street
and suddenly there was nothing
around me."

There is nothing around you.
You are an island.
The ocean is overbrimmed.
Sometimes it is too late
for anything else.

You said,
"I'll try to make it home,
but there's all that traffic."

"Okay," I said,
and I watched for you
and finally saw
your shadowed figure
come swimming homeward.

THE POEMS I HAVE LOST

She said to take the L-Train
to. . . .

I know where I left them—
on the floor of her apartment
with five locks on Thirteenth Street,
Somewhere Else City, USA.
I don't think I'll ever go back.

A young couple picked me up
east miles out of Asheville—
had just started a poem too—
and we stopped and smoked
at a roadside table
at the edge of June tobacco fields.
I lost them somewhere
between there and the Atlantic Ocean.

I wrote Duffie a long rambling
letter, called it a poem,
from Nashville, because
I got lonesome for sunsets
in Colorado Springtime and then
dropped the letter in the mailbox.
I wonder if it ever found her
in Juneau, Alaska.

The last thing I remember
was leaning into the roots
of a piñon tree. It wasn't
the horse that had thrown me;
it wasn't McCallister either
who owned the horse. It was
all that damn beer we had
been drinking all afternoon.

I got a letter from St. Paul, Minn.
inviting me up there to read poems.
I fell off the plane in Denver,
lost my ticket and most of my poems
but managed to hold on enough
to a few remaining things.

Memories, I guess they are,
crowd me because of all the signals
I've missed, the poems that keep
coming back in pieces.

Fragments remain with me, of course;
I touch the bare skeletons, smell
the old things, and see new visages pass
many, many times.
Those are enough.

HOW CLOSE

I wonder if I have ever come close
to seeing the first seed, the origin,
and where?

I've thought about it, says Coyote.

Once I thought I saw it in the glint
of a mica stratum a hairwidth deep.
I was a child then,
cradled in my mother's arm.
We were digging for the gray clay
to make pottery with.

That was south of Acoma years back;
that was the closest I've gotten yet.

I've thought about it, says Coyote.

LAST NIGHT

New York City almost got me
last night at Kennedy Airport.
So messed up,
making phone calls to places
I can't even remember.

Just held on tight
to my bag of poems, my life,
fighting off sleep,
the moments that swallow you
without your knowledge of where
you are disappearing to.

Finally, got a cab,
finally, got to a friend's place.
A phone call to you then,
lay on a carpet,
ate couple good apples,
drank glass of bourbon,
and it was already morning.
But, finally, I got to talk to you.
It was good, that part,
and I went to sleep on the floor
beside the phone
and two apple cores.

TODAY, THE A-TRAIN, 168th TO 14th

... The A-Train shakes bad
for this Indian.
I see blank faces, an old woman, a Black man,
somebody clutching a bag for her life.
I watch the numbers flashing by,
one blackness thunders into another,
another train crashes by headed uptown.
I can't even recognize anybody.

It is a relief to get off, and I walk,
trying to judge by the vague sun
which way I'm going, and I watch some construction
going on. I think of arbitration or something
like that, cross several streets and look
for the time, trying to make it meaningful.
I had even forgotten when it was
I was supposed to meet you.

HUNGER IN NEW YORK CITY

Hunger crawls into you
from somewhere out of your muscles
or the concrete or the land
or the wind pushing you.

It comes to you, asking
for food, words, wisdom, young memories
of places you ate at, drank cold spring water,
or held somebody's hand,
or home of the gentle, slow dances,
the songs, the strong gods, the world
you know.

That is, hunger searches you out.
It always asks you,
How are you, son? Where are you?
Have you eaten well?
Have you done what you as a person
of our people is supposed to do?

And the concrete of this city,
the oily wind, the blazing windows,
the shrieks of automation cannot,
truly cannot, answer for that hunger
although I have hungered,
truthfully and honestly, for them
to feed myself with.

So I sang to myself quietly:
I am feeding myself
with the humble presence
of all around me;
I am feeding myself
with your soul, my mother earth;
make me cool and humble.
Bless me.

TRAVELLED ALL THE WAY TO NEW YORK CITY

How are you?
Fine, and you?

It was good to touch you.

I liked your floppy black hat.

I liked that place we went to.
You had three beers,
I had three beers—
if I remember correctly.

I forgot to give you some sage
I had brought in a plastic bag.
I picked it in Arizona.
Next time, I'll remember.

That delicatessen was wild,
a real Jewish gourmet disneyland,
and I was like a little boy.
I could have stayed a long time.

You live in a nice place
even though you need five locks.

What was your cat's name?

Later, I said—an old line—
"I travelled all the way to New York
just to see you." Aaaiiieee!

Laughing, it's so good to laugh.

—Indian 1970 in NYC

FOR THOSE SISTERS & BROTHERS
IN GALLUP

He is that twisted shadow
under the bridge: he is
that broken root.

I know where he came from: I've
known you for so long
I want to take you home.

He got hit outside the city limits:
once
I saw a scatter of flesh and blood
mashed into the highway
east of Gallup.
           The car front wheels
shuddered over a lump,
and my body and soul shud-
dered, o my god.
           I turned
around up the road and drove
slowly back,
           o my god.
It was a dog left in tatters
of skin, splintered bone,
blood, and I dragged raggy meat
which was the leg and threw it
as hard
           and as far as I could
away from the Interstate
and prayed and moaned for us.

O my god, I know what is my name:
she stumbled like a stuffed dummy
against me, looked into my mouth
with her opaque remorseful eyes
and asked me for a drink.

I HAVE DRUNK AND TRIED TO KILL
MY ANGER IN YOUR GODDAMNED TOWN
AND I'M AFRAID FOR YOU AND ME
WHEN I WILL COME BACK AGAIN.

Be kind, sister, be kind;
it shall come cleansing again.
It shall rain and your eyes
will shine and look so deeply
into me into me into me into me.

EVENING BEACH WALK

I don't really feel like walking
at first
but somehow feel that I must
since I have come
this far
to this edge,
and so I walk.

The sun is going downwards
or rather one point changes to another,
and I know I am confronting
another horizon.

A dog comes sniffing at my knees
and I hold my hand to him,
and he sniffs, wags his tail
and trots away to join a young couple,
his friends, who smile as we meet.

I look many times as the sun sets
and I don't know why I can't see
clearly the horizon that I've imagined.

Maybe it's the clouds, the smog,
maybe it's the changing.

It's a duty with me,
I know, to find the horizons,
and I keep on walking on the ocean's edge,
looking for things in the dim light.

A PATIENCE POEM FOR THE CHILD THAT IS ME

Be patient child,
be patient, quiet.
The rivers run into the center
of the earth
and around
revolve all things
and flow
into the center.
Be patient, child,
quiet.

THE THIRD:
RETURNING

THE WISCONSIN HORSE

*It is late at night, lying
drunk on the floor, hearing
a church bell across the
street, remembering that
Wisconsin Horse
this Spring.*

One step at a time to return.

The horse across the road
stands within a fence,
silent in the hot afternoon.

A mile north is some construction.
I tell the horse,
"That's America building something."

A mile further through a clump of trees
is a river.

The Wisconsin Horse is silent.

The bell clamors
against the insides of my skull.
It has nothing to do with sound
that can comfort.

The clamor wants to escape
its barriers.
I want it to escape.
I have no defenses.

I should be an eager Christian
hungry for salvation,
or at the very least accept snugness
bound tightly in plastic.

Yet, at this single point in my life,
I know only a few bare things:
the floor, the walls around me,
that bell across the street,
that despair is a miserable excuse
for emptiness,
that I should echo louder
that call for salvation
which at this point I know
is a need to fill the hollows
and pockets of my body.

Despair is such a poor excuse
to exclude things from my life,
to allow them to slip
from safe places.

    But now, and not too soon,
in this dark night,
having gotten up to write,
I make this offering:
that Wisconsin Horse I saw
standing in the hot afternoon,
staring through a chainlink fence
at the construction going on
only a mile away,
I wonder now
if the horse still stands
silent in the dark night,
dreamless and stifled,
having no recourses left
except to hope his silence
will soon go away
and the meaningfulness enter.

A BARROOM FRAGMENT

He was talking,
"I invited her to Las Vegas,
and when we got to the hotel
she asked for a separate room.
I told her, 'Shit, if you want
a room to yourself, why baby
that's alright, have it.'
I had brought her up there
on a four-million-dollar airplane,
and I told her, 'You can
go across the street
and take a thirty-thousand-dollar bus
back to Burbank.'"
That was Coyote talking.

FOUR YEARS AGO

Four years ago
I was in Wisconsin
somewhere,
making for the stateline,
crossing,
heading homewards.
I wondered
in what period of history
I was then.

I wonder that now.

Yesterday,
I told my wife,
"You must see me
in the perspective
of my whole life."

It all adds
ups and downs.

HORIZONS AND RAINS

Interstate 40 from Albuquerque
to Gallup—
witness to the brown people
stumbling Sunday afternoon
northwards—

    "Where's the rain that feels so good?"

and to Tsaile, the mountains, dark buttes—

"Maybe if the Hopis and Navajos quit
messing around," Ackley says.

    "Where it has always been."

The brown people losing trails
and finding trails and losing them
and finding again—

the horizons
and rains
in the far distance.

LEAVING AMERICA

That time in Kansas City bus depot,
met Roy.

"Yaahteh, shikis."
"Where you from?"
"Arizona."
"Where you coming from?"
"Moline."

Jus' got paid,
laid off by the Rock Island Line.

Going home.
It's got red and brown land,
sage, and when it rains,
it smells like piñon
and pretty girls at a Squaw Dance.

I know.

WASHYUMA MOTOR HOTEL

Beneath the cement foundations
of the motel, the ancient spirits
of the people conspire sacred tricks.
They tell stories and jokes and laugh
and laugh.

The American passersby
get out of their hot, stuffy cars
at evening, pay their money wordlessly,
and fall asleep without benefit of dreams.
The next morning, they get up,
dress automatically, brush their teeth,
get in their cars and drive away.
They haven't noticed that the cement
foundations of the motor hotel
are crumbling, bit by bit.

The ancient spirits tell stories
and jokes and laugh and laugh.

PASSING THROUGH LITTLE ROCK

The old Indian ghosts—
                    "Quapaw"
"Waccamaw"—
                    are just billboard words
in this crummy town.

"You know, I'm worrying a lot lately,"
he says in the old hotel bar.

"You're getting older and scared ain't you?"

I just want to cross the next hill,
through that clump of trees
and come out the other side

and see a clean river,
the whole earth new
and hear the noise it makes
at birth.

SOMETIMES IT'S BETTER TO LAUGH, "HONEST INJUN"

Chicago O'Hare Field

You're Indian aren't you? this slim man
with a weak face asks me in a conspiring voice.
Yes, I nod. And he shows me a belt buckle.
Handmade, he tells me, but someone told me
that it was phony turquoise
and plastic records, junk.

I look at it, and it is plastic,
paste turquoise and shiny aluminum,
and I tell him, You may be right,
you know that?

You can't trust anybody these days,
he says. And he gets sullen, says,
Got it in Flagstaff, know a lot of Indians
and I even know some in Wyoming.
They told me this was genuine, handmade,
but you can't trust anybody these days,
not even an honest injun.

He shows me a business card,
looks around with his shallow eyes.
It reads: Jackson Arms Corp.
          Jim Penning, Pres.
          Jackson Hole, Wyoming
He tells me in a low voice, I'm working
on a high frequency sound machine,
above human hearing. You ought to see
the way it works; it's neat.
It can really destroy things,
blow them apart just like that.
The laser ain't nothing. I'm working on it,
he reassures me. I nod my head,
but I'm not reassured, and I don't really
want to see the way it works, neatly.

[63]

I continue to drink my beer,
wondering about this weak-faced man
who is conspiring with me,
telling me his horrible secret,
this man whom an Indian sold a piece
of junk jewelry. Maybe that's why
he's pissed off and he's been working
on a weapon to recoup his foolish purchase
and by his revelation to include me
in his conscience.

I ask him, Why? then. His eyes turn cloudy,
and he mumbles into his drink.
He doesn't know perhaps,
and he doesn't want to conspire
with me anymore, probably fearing
that I will sell him
another piece of "genuine" jewelry.

I finish my beer, take a look
at O'Hare TV schedule monitors,
checking for departure announcement
but it's not there yet, and I walk
anyway into the concourse tunnel
for Gate 11-B and decide to laugh
my deep relief. And it's all true.

MISSING THAT INDIAN NAME OF ROY OR RAY

1.

Can't even remember his name.
Maybe it was Roy or Ray—
tell Leslie that.
Drinking on Des Moines-to-K.C. bus,
throbbing with dull nerves,
going home, coming home,
talk to nobody until K.C. depot.

He's wobbling down from Chicago bus
first I see him.
"Yaahteh, where you from?"
"Sanders."
I know where Sanders is,
west of Gallup right off U.S. 66.
Roy, Navajo, coming from places.
New levis, new shirt, new everything,
just got laid off the Rock Island Line.
Right in style, man, don't talk English
too good, but that's okay,
expensive transistor radio we listen to.
That's okay, shikis,
I like cowboy music, sentimental crap,
go to dances at Milan's in Gallup,
saw somebody getting laid out in back once,
saw somebody get knifed there too.
Red blood black and shiny in neon light,
quick footsteps running away,
me and my buddy careful to approach him,
don't touch him, and then make a phone call.

In Kansas City bus depot,
two Indians going for a drink.
Wink at barmaid, two whiskies, two beers
settle down warm but in a hurry.
Look for danger.

Later on in the bus, he sings Navajo songs.
Indians singing, you sing
when there's a crowd, girls,
and fires that smell good.
    "Give me two dollars.
        And I will like you."
A Black guy and a hippie girl
come and join us in the back.
    "No more dollar.
        No more dollar."

In the early morning,
when it's getting light,
we're outside of Tulsa, and you see
those oil wells, pumping the juice,
nodding all the time, up and down,
up and down, all day, getting rich.
On the outskirts, we see a sign:
Tulsa Screw Products, Co.,
and we laugh and laugh.

2.

He gets lost in Amarillo.
Went to get a couple hamburgers
and then didn't show back up.
"Where's that Indian that was back here?"
the bus driver asks.
"Went to get some hamburgers," I tell him,
and then I run around the block
but can't find him;
at least he took his expensive radio with him.
Me and the Black guy and the hippie girl
keep looking out the back window
when we pull out of Amarillo.

3.

The Black guy gets off in Tucumcari,
and I wonder that it's a strange place
for a Black man to get off at,
Tucumcari, New Mexico.

4.

When I get off in Albuquerque,
the girl stays on.
"See you in Portland," she says.
And I walk up the street
missing that Indian we left behind
in Amarillo.

CROSSING THE COLORADO RIVER INTO YUMA

It is almost dusk.

For a long time,
we've been travelling.

I saw a hawk
flying low against the sky.
The horizon was stone.

That was only a while back.

No one owns this river. Wash with it. Drink it.
Water your plants with it. Pray with it.

The evening sun glimmers across the desert.

Colors signal memories
of past journeys.

Sounds filled everything
and overflowed
upon returning.

Now, the river is silent.

The Greyhound bus roars smoothly on the bridge.
The river bed is hot sand.
The willows are last weak vestiges.
Alongside the river bed is a concrete canal.
The liquid in it flows swiftly, directed, and lifeless.

A brown man leans
by the Yuma bus depot wall;
a daze is in his eyes.

He tries and tries
to smell the river.

He leans,
trying to feel welcomed
to his home.

Yuma is a small town.
It abounds with modern Americana,
motels, gas stations, schools, churches, and etc. Where
did they all come from?
Do they really plan for survival this way?

Neon is weak.

Concrete will soon return
to desert.

Be patient, child, be kind
and not bitter.

Prepare for the morning.
Go down to the river bed.
It will let you.

Sing a bit, be patient.
Wait.

VALLEY OF THE SUN

Where's the sun that feels so good?

Tired, nauseous in belly, breathe
the sandy wind at a roadside stop near Phoenix.
My son whimpers.
                    We had travelled
from the Grand Canyon where we had awoken,
down through Prescott early in the morning
of Christmas Day. Nobody seemed awake;
it was a calm and deserted town.

I searched for a road to Skull Valley
where I'd spent one year of a boyhood.
Down through the mountains, a winding road,
recognized places where I learned to smoke,
consider enticing thoughts, to read,
explored and where I'd almost gotten laid
on a hillside in a barn, an old musty barn
with useless hay. Later, I climbed down
into the sunlight, that knowledge trembling
in my mind, a boy growing for manhood.

Where's the sun that feels so good?

A dim sun led us into Phoenix, the Valley
of the Sun, passed by John Jacob's Farm
where the lettuce grows in such sterile lines.
They are taking the water with machines
out of the river, in fact, setting the course
of rivers, and they make artificial rain.

The
      sunlight
              is so
                    dim,
passing by John Jacob's Farm.
We look for life. Look, but there are only lines
of lettuce converging at the far end.

[69]

Where's the Sun that feels so good?

There are stories about Montezuma.
He came from the south, a magnificent man,
a warrior, a saint, generous and gentle.
He carried a golden cane, they say,
and touching earth, green things would spring up,
and he led animals and people to water
he tapped out of solid stone.
There are these stories.

A DYING WARRIOR

Leonard Bluebird,
she tells me in Smitty's Bar,
sobbing immense sorrow,
is dying of leukemia.
I can't do nothing for him.
Look, he's limping.

The dying Leonard is wobbling
across the floor, dancing, drunk.
The music is crude and loud
and cowboy.
Many Indians staring.

O I can't look, she says.
He's got a sister,
but she can't do anything.
I'm the same way.
He doesn't want to die
in the Indian Hospital.

I step out into the night
concrete cliffed Phoenix,
sad and walking, cussing
at the streets and the dying bird.

I TOLD YOU I LIKE INDIANS

You meet Indians everywhere.

Once, I walked into this place—
Flagler Beach, Florida,
you'd never expect it—
a bar; some old people ran it.

The usual question, of course,
"You're an Indian, aren't you?"
"Yes, ma'am." I'm Indian alright.
Wild, ignorant, savage!
And she wants me to dance.
Well, okay, been drinking beer
all the way from Hollywood.
We dance something.

You're Indian aren't you?
Yeah, jeesus christ almighty,
I'm one of them.

I like Indians!

"There's an Indian around here."
What? And in walks a big Sioux.
Crissake man, how's relocation, brother?
He shakes my hand. Glad to see you.
I thought I was somewhere else.
We play the pingpong machine, drink beer,
once in a while dance with the old lady
who likes Indians.

I like Indians!

I *told* you
You meet Indians everywhere.

THE SIGNIFICANCE OF A
VETERAN'S DAY

I happen to be a veteran
but you can't tell in how many ways
unless I tell you.

A cold morning waking up on concrete;
I never knew that feeling before,
calling for significance,
and no one answered.

Let me explain it this way
so that you may not go away
without knowing a part of me:

that I am a veteran of at least 30,000 years
when I travelled with the monumental yearning
of glaciers, relieving myself by them,
growing, my children seeking shelter
by the roots of pines and mountains.

When it was that time to build,
my grandfather said, "We cut stone and mixed mud
and ate beans and squash and sang
while we moved ourselves. That's what we did."
And I believe him.

And then later on in the ancient and deep story
of all our nights, we contemplated,
contemplated not the completion of our age,
but the continuance of the universe,
the travelling, not the progress,
but the humility of our being there.

Caught now, in the midst of wars
against foreign disease, missionaries,
canned food, Dick & Jane textbooks, IBM cards,
Western philosophies, General Electric,
I am talking about how we have been able
to survive insignificance.

TO & FRO

On the train to California,
a Black porter told me,
"We don't serve Indians hard liquor, chief."
I said, "That's okay, man."
When I got home my wife asked,
"What are you doing back here?"
I said, "I came home."

Actually, I was a fugitive.
I had decided that at 8:00 A.M.
in the East Commons
over scalding coffee, sitting
at an imitation-wood table
as I watched crowds of students
mangle each other before breakfast.

I had several strange moments
thinking of Charles Olson
and language, thinking about a point
in particular the night before
when the night and the connections
were one and the same,
and I had touched a sustaining motion,
realizing the energy that language is
and becomes.

I had to leave California
I told my wife later
but kept secret that dove I heard
one precarious morning
when I was sick and moaned for home,
pushing back the memory of a boy
in Summer morning fields.

FRAGMENT

On my way to city court
to be judged again,
I pick up a small stone.

The month is March;
it will be Easter soon.
I put the stone in my pocket;
it is that I feel the need
for deliverance and maybe
if I do this.

My hands are sweaty;
my fervent vain wish
is that I had never
been in jail
that first time.

I put the stone in my other hand
and caress it with my fingertips.
I find it is moist
and realize it is a fragment
of the earth center
and I know that it is
my redemption.

NOTES ON THE STEPS OF THE SAN DIEGO BUS DEPOT

Across the street
America is putting together
another Federal Building.

The Wisconsin Horse
looks through the chainlink fence.
He turns and tells me with his eyes.

I discover Marge Piercy
in a poetry newspaper.
Her thick sensual lips
are about to move
upon the earth.
I wonder if her dark eyes
are always seeing
beyond the farthest ridge.
Her words slant into me
and resonate
and will echo
for a long time.
For centuries maybe.

I don't think the sky will fall today,
but I need a few surprises badly.

EAST OF SAN DIEGO

I tell the bus driver
but he doesn't hear,
"Keep to the hills
and avoid America
if you can.
I'm a fugitive
from bad, futureless dreams
in Southern California."

CROW

"Did you see any crows
in San Diego?"

One, once in the desert
southeast of San Diego,
watched as he slid
on his wind road
across the valley
towards El Centro,
probably stopped
that night
by the Salton Sea.
I wondered how
he made it look so easy.

RETURNED FROM CALIFORNIA

At the park
yesterday afternoon,
I found a dead crow
by the roots of a cottonwood.

Death is a bundle
of black feathers,
leather-lined dry holes
for eyes,
withered yellow feet.

Other crows
hollered from branches
above a scatter
of human garbage.
They forget easy enough.

Right now, I'm too tired
to scheme things,
but that will return
soon enough.
Dreams gather quickly
like Spring crows,
and they scatter.

PAIN

Sometimes there's the slow,
slow unnecessary hurt.
My poor body is being devoured;
it is disintegrating.
The twinge comes from under,
tears the sacred flesh given me,
leaves no seeds for regeneration.
I should have taken her advice.
"You know, you should stay here
a long time by this ocean
and just sit and listen."

WIND AND GLACIER VOICES

Laguna man said,
I only heard that glacier scraping
once, thirty thousand years ago.
My daughter was born then.
                    —a storytelling, continuing
                        voice—

West of Yuma, a brown man murmurs
the motion of the solar wind.
                    —a harsh, searing
                        voice—

Please don't tell me
how to live;
I've always lived this way.
                    —a protesting
                        voice—

The last time I was in Fargo
I thought I heard the echo
of a glacier scraping.

                    —a remembering,
                      beckoning
                      voice—

And the wind, solar,
the big wind will come.
Solar, it will come.
It will pass by and through
and with everything.

                    —a longing, whispering,
                      prophetic
                      voice—

ALBUQERQUE BACK AGAIN: 12/6/74

After leaving Joy at class,
Rainy falls asleep
on the way back to the house.
Her head droops,
and I pull parka hood carefully
around her head.
Small round face, the wind
catches black hair,
puppy hair.
She sleeps, this child—
never mind the traffic
and ordinary insanity
of people going places
they might not actually know
the destinations of.

Day with blue sky,
cloud fluffs.
          Look to see
the mountains, and they are there,
the late Autumn sun sketching
crags and shadows, knife edge
of stone and granite ridge.

Yesterday, turning south
for New Mexico at San Luis,
Coyote looked at the mountains
and said, "We'll see you again."
And prayed for safety, strength,
and the ability to see beauty.
It was beginning to snow then.

EAST OF TUCUMCARI

I asked to get off
sixteen miles east of Tucumcari,
and the busdriver asked,
"Where are you going?"

I was coming home.

I saw the brown water
falling from a rock.
It felt so good
to touch the green moss.
A woman between
the mountain ridges
of herself—
it is overwhelming.

I could even smell
the northern mountains
in the water.

WATCHING YOU

For Joy

I watch you
from the gentle slope
where it is warm
by your shoulder.
My eyes are closed.
I can feel the tap
of your blood
against my cheek.
Inside my mind,
I see the gentle move
ment of your valleys,
the undulations
of slow turnings.
Opening my eyes,
there is a soft dark
and beautiful butte
moving up and then down
as you breathe.
There are fine
and very tiny ferns
growing, and I can
make them move
by breathing.
I watch you with my skin
moving upon yours,
and I have known you well.

BEND IN THE RIVER

Flicker flies by.
His ochre wing
is tied to prayer sticks.
Pray for mountains,
the cold strong shelter.

Sun helps me to see
where Arkansas River
ripples over pebbles.
Glacial stone moves slowly;
it will take a while.

A sandbank cuts sharply
down to a poplar log
buried in damp sand.
Shadow lengths tell me
it is afternoon.

There are tracks
at river's edge, raccoon,
coyote, deer, crow,
and now my own.

My sight follows
the river upstream
until it bends.
Beyond the bend
is more river
and, soon, the mountains.
We shall arrive,
to see, soon.

THE FOURTH:

THE RAIN FALLS

EARTH WOMAN

for Joy

This woman has been shaping
mountains
millions of years and still
her volcanoes erupt
with continuous mysteries.

How gentle
her movements, her hands,
soft wind,
warm rain,
the moving pain
of pleasure

we share.

SPREADING WINGS ON WIND

*a plane ride from Rough
Rock to Phoenix Winter
Indian 1969*

I must remember
that I am only one part
among many parts,
not a singular eagle
or one mountain. I am
a transparent breathing.

Below are dark lines of stone,
fluff of trees, mountains
and the Earth's People—all of it,
the Feather in a prayer.

Faint, misty clouds,
a sudden turbulence,
and steady, the solid earth.

"It looks like a good road,"
from Piñon to Low Mountain.
It branches off to First Mesa
and then Second and Third Mesa.

The Hopi humanity
which is theirs and ours.

Three of the Navajo Mountains
in our vision, "Those mountains
over there, see their darkness
and strength, full of legends,
heroes, trees, the wind, sun."

East, West, North, and South.
Those Directions and Mountains.
Mountain Taylor, San Francisco Peak,
Navajo Mountain, Dibentsaa.
The Navajo mind must have been
an eagle that time.

Breathe like this on the feather
and cornfood like this, this way.

Sometime before there were billboards
advertising Meteor Crater,
there must have been one hell of a jolt,
flame and then silence.
After many years, flowers and squirrels,
snow streaking down inside the cone.

Over Winslow is the question,
"Who the hell was Winslow, some cowboy?"
A miner? Surveyor? Missionary?
The forests are neatly trimmed hedges;
mines are feeble clawings at the earth.

What the hell are you doing to this land?
My grandfather hunted here, prayed,
dreamt; one day there was a big jolt,
flame, and then silence,
just the clouds forming.

FOR NANAO

*a Japanese friend poet who
visited Canyon de Chelley*

That time you came back
and told us
about meeting a Navajo woman
on the canyon's rim,
you were happy and smiling.

You said, "We were talking,
smiling and gesturing to each."

Yes, Nanao,
you must have been truly.

The two languages,
Navajo and Japanese,
origins from the monumental age
of glacial Asia,
it is all true.

You must have been
mother and son then,
or sister and brother,
or lover and lover.

I can see you smiling,
remembering that time
in millennia. I can see
the lights in your eyes.

THE BOY AND COYOTE

for a friend, Ed Theis, met
at VAH, Ft. Lyons,
Colorado, November and
December 1974

You can see the rippled sand rifts
shallow inches below the surface.
I walk on the alkalied sand.
Willows crowd the edges of sand banks
sloping to the Arkansas River.

I get lonesome for the young afternoons
of a boy growing at Acoma.
He listens to the river,
the slightest nuance of sound.

Breaking thin ice from a small still pool,
I find Coyote's footprints.
Coyote, he's always somewhere before you;
he knows you'll come along soon.
I smile at his tracks which are not fresh
except in memory and say a brief prayer
for goodluck for him and for me and thanks.

All of a sudden, and not far away,
there are the reports of a shotgun,
muffled flat by saltcedar thickets.
Everything halts for several moments,
no sound; even the wind holds to itself.
The animal in me crouches, poised immobile,
eyes trained on the distance, waiting
for motion again. The sky is wide;
blue is depthless; and the animal
and I wait for breaks in the horizon.

Coyote's preference is for silence
broken only by the subtle wind,
uncanny bird sounds, saltcedar scraping,
and the desire to let that man free,
to listen for the motion of sound.

MY CHILDREN, AND A PRAYER FOR US

Raho says, "You take a feather
and this white stuff,
and you let it fall to the ground;
that's praising."
Yes, son, it is,
and your words will always
remain like that.
Be strong and think clear thoughts,
always see the wholeness
of what is around you,
touch their realness,
feel the vibrating motion
of mornings,
exult in your presence
with the humility
that true knowledge imparts,
that you are one part
among many and all parts.

Rainy
daughter dark eyes
touch wind quiver
the inwards of mountain power
full flow
know the innate tension
that is your life
in stones leaves insects
lights in frost crystals;
simple words I wish
for you
ours to share.

Allspirit, pray with me
my humble prayers: I give you
myself, my only hope I know,
knowing nothing else
except that I have truly nothing
to offer except that which
you have given to me;
I give it back to you.

Thank you.

FOUR DHEETSIYAMA POEMS

I wake this morning to snow,
snow everywhere
and a heavy dry mist
which begins to clear
around 8:30.
Outside is a bitter
windless bite
on ears and cheeks,
and the snow is powdery dry,
drifted where the wind
has blown it.
"It snowed on Saturday,"
my mother and father tell me
and describe their stay
last week at Acu helping
with the Winterprayers.
My mother says, "We got cold
the other night because
the door had opened
during the night.

I had felt cold
and I got up once
to put wood in the stove
and went back to bed.
Later, I was cold again
and getting up to build the fire
I saw light coming in
through the door.
It was already getting morning.
Looking over at your father
who was sleeping by the west wall,
I called to him,
but he didn't answer.
Checking his bed, I found him
all rolled up in his blankets,
and I told him that the door
must have opened and there was snow
drifted inside the house.
No wonder we were so cold,"
she says, and we all laugh.

It's good in the morning
to eat breakfast
with my mother and my father,
drink hot coffee,
see the morning life.
My nephews and my nieces
are going to school;
they run through the snow,
puffs of snow kicking
off their shoes,
running for the school bus.
On this cold morning,
Louise's husband starts cars,
first Louise's, then Myrna's,
and then Aunt Katie's.
After a while, they all leave.
The sky is very clear winter blue.

Looking north and seeing
Kaweshtima, the strong mountain
is a prayer.
On cold winter days, the mountain
seems taller and bigger,
the distinctions made by the contrast
of light and dark, the differences
made sharper and clearer,
the clarity of space.
It occurs to me again
that wherever I have been,
I have never seen a Mountain
that has stood so clearly
in my mind; when I have needed
to envision my home, when loneliness
for myself has overcome me,
the Mountain has occurred.
Now, I see it sharing its being
with me, praying.

On Friday, Joy and I talked
about sense of presence.
What is it? How does it come about?
I think it has to do
with a sense of worth, dignity,
and how you fit with occasion, place,
people, and time.
It's also a physical thing,
carriage of body,
hand and head movements,
eyes fixed upon specific points.
And then it is an ability
which is instinctive and spiritual
to convey what you see
to those around you.
Essentially, it is how you fit
into that space which is yourself,
how well and appropriately.

MY MOTHER AND MY SISTERS

My oldest sister wears thick glasses
because she can't see very well.
She makes beautifully formed pottery.
That's the thing about making dhyuuni;
it has to do more with a sense of touching
than with seeing because fingers
have to know the texture of clay
and how the pottery is formed from lines
of shale strata and earth movements.
The pottery she makes is thinwalled
and has a fragile but definite balance.
In other words, her pottery has a true ring
when it is tapped with a finger knuckle.

Here, you try it;
you'll know what I mean.

The design that my mother is painting
onto the bowl is done with a yucca stem brush.
My other sister says, "Our mother,
she can always tell when someone else has used
a brush that she is working with," because
she has chewed it and made it into her own way.
She paints with movements whose origin
has only to do with years of knowing
just the right consistency of paint,
the tensile vibrancy of the yucca stem,
and the design that things are supposed to have.

She can always tell.

My mother talks about one time.
"One time, my sister and I
and this one lady—she was
a fat woman—went to roast piñons.

Stuwahmeeskuunaati, over that way."
To the east of Acu the mesa cliffs
are red, brown, and white sandstone;
there are piñon trees there.
"We left in the morning
and walked up to the first level,
not on top, where there was a lot
of piñons that year.
We had to get the piñons
in their cones from the trees
and dig a hole and bury them
and then build a fire on top.
It took quite a while
to do that, like it does.
And then we got them out
and let them cool,
and then we gathered them
up and put them on our backs
in sacks. We started back
to Acu." It's a long ways
across the valley, sandhills,
grasses, brush, cottonwoods,
gullies, cacti. "When we got
to this one place, the woman said,
'This is where Maashadruwee lives.
You have to holler.'
You're supposed to yell or holler.
We prayed with cornmeal
and the lady said, 'Please,
Maashadruwee, make Acu closer
to us.' And we started again,
but before we got to Acu
onto the south trail,
it grew dark.
We knew that our relatives
would worry about us.
And sure enough, the woman's husband
was looking and he met us
at the bottom of the trail.

When we got to south of the church,
my father met us—he had come
to look for us too."
My mother chuckles with the memory
of it, when she was a young girl.
"I don't know if my sister
remembers, but I do, very clearly.
But I don't know
what my age was then."

WHAT JOY SAID ON TWO OCCASIONS

One of our neighbors is a young man
with one leg thinner and shorter
than the other, and a couple of weeks ago
I saw him pouring charcoal fluid
on an anthill several yards from his door,
and then he set fire to it.
Walking over to him I said,
"Why you doing that for, man?"

Charcoal fluid and burning ants smell ugly.
I told Joy about it.
A couple of days ago
that guy was limping towards his door,
and I said that he must have the limp
because he had polio as a child.

Joy said, "It's probably because
he burns ants."
It's probably because she's Creek
that makes her know that.

This morning, while I was waking up,
she said, "I got up and went back to bed
two times. When I get up now,
it's almost still dark."

Later, when I got up and it was quiet,
I looked out that window that I busted
one night when I was drunk,
and outside was so clear and good
that I felt lonely for all those things
I haven't done lately.

JUANITA, WIFE OF MANUELITO

*after seeing a photograph
of her in Dine Baa-Hani*

I can see by your eyes
the gray in them like by Sonsela Butte,
the long ache
that comes about when I think
about where the road climbs
up onto the Roof Butte.

I can see
the whole sky
when it is ready to rain
over Whiskey Creek,
and a small girl
driving her sheep
and she looks so pretty
her hair tied up
with a length of yarn.

I can see
by the way you stare
out of a photograph
that you are a stern woman
informed by the history
of a long walk
and how it must have felt
to leave the canyons
and the mountains of your own land.

I can see, Navajo woman,
that it is possible for dreams
to occur, the prayers full of the mystery
of children, laughter, the dances,
my own humanity, so it can last unto forever.

That is what I want to teach my son.

A PRETTY WOMAN

We came to the edge
of the mesa
and looked below.

We could see
the shallow wash
snaking down
from the cut
between two mesas,
all the way from Black Mountain;

and the cottonwoods
from that distance
looked like a string of turquoise,

and the land was a pretty woman
smiling at us
looking at her.

BONY

My father brought that dog home
in a gunny sack.

The reason we called it Bony
was because it was skin and bones.

It was a congenital problem
or something that went way back
in its dog's history.

We loved it without question,
its history and ours.

TWO ACOMA PICTURES

LITTLE WREN I NEED A SONG

Little Wren, this morning, quickly
make me a song
made of sandstone clefts,
a bit of yucca growing there.
Quickly, my friend, just a bit
of song which goes:
      cool morning shadow
      sandstone ledge mica glints
      sun will rise from Chuska horizon.

TWO WOMEN AT THE NORTHERN CISTERN

Tadpole says,
      Where were you last night.
      I was waiting for you all night.
      I know you think I am still young.
      But I am getting bigger; watch.

      Here, drink from my well.

FOR RAINY'S BOOK

Poetry is
the silence
of Sun and Quuti.

A DEER DINNER

After you have gotten a deer,
a dinner is given for it.
Kudra quuya comes to the dinner,
and she acts like a silly old gal.
She teases with you
like you were her man, making promises.
And then she takes the eyes
out of the deer's head
which is boiling in a big pot.
And then she blesses you with prayer
for your virility and goodluck
and not to disappoint her promises.

A SNOWY MOUNTAIN SONG

I like her like that,

a white scarf
tied to her head,
the lines on her face
are strong.

Look, the snowy mountain.

YUUSTHIWA

"Whenever people are driving along and stop
to offer Yuusthiwa a ride, he refuses
and says, 'I still have my legs,' "
my father says, saying it like the old man,
a slow careful drawl. And my mother corrects him,
" 'While I'm still able to walk.' "
Yuusthiwa has been sick lately;
either something fell on him
or else he got bit by something, she heard.
Apparently, he still gets around though
pretty much because like my father says
one fellow had said, " 'That old man,
he's still tom-catting around, visiting.'
You see him in Acomita along the road
or in McCartys." I chuckle at the expression
picturing the old guy in mind; after all,
Yuusthiwa is only 114 years old at last count.

"One time, David and I were coming
from Acomita," my father says, "and we stopped
for him. Recognizing me, he got in and said
'Ahku Tsai-rrhlai kudha." And as we drove
westwards up this way, he told us things.
I had asked him, 'Naishtiya, how do you come
to live as many years as you have, to be so fortunate
as to mature as healthy and firm as you are?'
And he said, 'If you live enjoying and appreciating
your life, taking care of yourself, caring for
and being friendly with others; if you use the plants
that grow around here, seeing and knowing
that they are of use, boiling them into medicine
to use in the right way in caring for yourself,
cleansing and helping your body with them;
that's the way I have lived.' That's the way
he said it," my father says.

HAWK

Hawk
sweeps
clear through
the background
which is sky
and mountain ledge.
—Old Chuska Mountain,
my friend, shelter—
His immense knowledge
of wind,
his perception
of circling slow wind,
his edge of wing
on air trail

straightens then suddenly
overhead,
directly above us,
the pines.

This man, he knows
what he is doing.

BUZZARD

Climbing suddenly
out of a ravine,
we saw a black buzzard
working at carrion.
The air was rancid,
not much wind,
and the dust was hot
and still, like the day.

Quietly now, pull
the breath back
into the body.

Sky is very endless
and dry; no clouds.

The buzzard doesn't see
us as it pokes
upon the animal wreckage,
rags of skin and entrails,
poor bones, claws.

Suddenly, the wind shifts,
air changes, and dust
sweeps to the bird,
and it looks toward us,
suddenly fearful, the briefest
recognition in its eyes,

and then with a great clatter
of wings, it rushes
away, a torn entrail sodden
with rot falls behind it
into the dust.

Breath is let out,
and the hot wind reeks again.

I've heard an older man say, "They take the eyes first."
I wonder why? I think it must have to do with ritual,
some distinct memory consistent with the history of its
preceding generations. And the buzzard pays ritual
homage to the memory of its line, the tradition that
insures that things will continue. Yes, that must be
what it is. Eyes have a quality of regenerating visions
which must continue first and last of all.

DRY ROOT IN A WASH

The sand is fine grit
and warm to the touch.
An old juniper root
lies by the cutbank of sand;
it lingers, waiting
for the next month of rain.

I feel like saying,
It will rain, but you know
better than I these centuries
don't mean much
for anyone to be waiting.

Upstream, towards the mountains,
the Shiwana work for rain.

They know we're waiting.

Underneath the fine sand
it is cool
with crystalline moisture,
the forming rain.

CURLY MUSTACHE, 101-YEAR-OLD
NAVAJO MAN

Thin, strong man.
Wears glasses
with stretch band
knotted behind head.
White mustache
hangs long
sides of mouth.

How long this cricket
been around?

Gray hat hangs
from chair armrest
at his side.

Motions
with long hand,
brown fingers
shape the mountain
ridge
of his knuckles.
Meadow wind
flows in channels
of his skin.

How many times
the mountain tops?
How many times
the roots?

Wears Penney's neoprene
soled ankle-high boots.

Voice is wind
down canyon—
tiny headwater wind
from beneath granite
onto flat plain—
soothing cool wind.

A thousands of years
old cicada
here one moment,
one place
in millennia

Tell me about glaciers.
Tell me if this is correct
what I have heard: the scrape
of a glacier sounds
like a touching wind
on stone, wood,
in someplace mountain dream.
I heard it from a Laguna man.
"A returning noise," he said,
"I got the story
from someone way back."

Old man, he points
with the old root,
the compass
of his hand knows
the waterholes,
watercourses,
the life flow
on earth places
of his mind.

FOUR RAINS

for my daughter,
Rainy Dawn

First Rain

She looks at me
so brighteyed I can
see
so far
the mountains shining
when light slants
through rain
into roots
so delicate
they will probably last
always last.

Second Rain

Voice
begins this way,
pointing things out.
I know that you will
listen for sounds
only you will
understand
the way they mean
to me.

Third Rain

Brighteyed flash,
the tiniest mirrored
dreams reaching back
into granite who know
magic and mysteries;
there they are.
There.

FOURTH RAIN

Don't misunderstand me,
Shiwana.
She's my daughter.
I know what she's saying.
I know her name;
I know.

MORNING STAR

The space before dawn
holds morning star
in its true eye,
the center of all places
looking out
and always in,

the mountain shale
of still deep night
is all light
yet undiscovered,
solid and single,
a glacier without motion
until the gleam
of eternal orbits
shall be complete
and be alive,

for the morning star
finds that dawn
on its journey
through our single being,
the all that has depth
and completeness,
the single eye
through which we see
and are seen.

A STORY OF HOW A WALL STANDS

At Acu, there is a wall
almost 400 years old
which supports hundreds
of tons of dirt and bones—
it's a graveyard built on a
steep incline—and it looks
like it's about to fall down
the incline but will not for
a long time.

My father, who works with stone,
says, "That's just the part you see,
the stones which seem to be
just packed in on the outside,"
and with his hands puts the stone and mud
in place. "Underneath
what looks like loose stone,
there is stone woven together."
He ties one hand over the other,
fitting like the bones of his hands
and fingers. "That's what is
holding it together."

"It is built that carefully,"
he says, "the mud mixed
to a certain texture," patiently
"with the fingers," worked
in the palm of his hand. "So that
placed between the stones, they hold
together for a long, long time."

He tells me those things,
the story of them worked
with his fingers, in the palm
of his hands, working the stone
and the mud until they become
the wall that stands a long, long time.

FOR JOY TO LEAVE UPON

December 28, 1974

Last night a bit before six,
walking from the river,
I saw my shadow by the moonlight.
Broken by the slight rise of a small hill,
ankle-high plants, earth imprints.
Had walked down to the old pear tree,
winter barren, stepped over loosened wire fence.
(Remembered one Autumn early evening
when I killed a flicker for feathers.
Wounded the bird with an airgun,
broke its wing. Flopping running bird
through underbrush, and when I caught it
I had to press its tight neck with my finger
and thumb. The warm struggle of muscle,
feathers, blood upon my skin, its gray eye,
the intense moments of a boy twelve years old.)

Fell once on snow and damp earth,
muscle pulled, sore for a while only though
and now can't tell which shoulder it was
I fell upon, the memory of pain gone.

The reflection of the silver moon
was broken on the river; it was a whipping flag.

The year I got out of the Army,
I tried to see if my grandfather's grapevines
would ever grow again.
I cut the dead vines down to the quick
of the main stem, inches above cluster of roots,
(piled dry gray vines and burned them—
smoke is sweet and acrid) and pulled dirt
in circles around the roots and watered them.
But I left that Summer. Later,
I came back and saw a few green new shoots,
and then I left again.

Tonight, there is a waning moon.

IT DOESN'T END, OF COURSE

for Adelle, Spring 1970

It doesn't end.

In all growing
from all earths
to all skies,

in all touching
all things,

in all soothing
the aches of all years,

it doesn't end.